The *Exodus*

Where New Beginnings Happen

Nancy Yarbrough-Banks

The *Exodus*
Where New Beginnings Happen

ISBN: 978-1-7341169-1-5

Library of Congress Control Number: 2019916765

Printed in the United States of America

T.A.L.K. Publishing, LLC

Talkconsulting.net

Acknowledgments

Russell

My firstborn son, when I look at you, it reminds me of what Strength, Resilience, and Dedication look like.

Robbie

You have taught me so much about what a mother should or could be by watching you raise my 4 beautiful grandsons.

Quintin

When I look at you, it reminds me that love can conquer all things.

Keyara

My mini-me when God made you, He broke the mold. When I look at you, I know that part of me lived.

Destiny

You are and have always been destined to do great things in God.

Rodney

My husband, my love, my modern-day Boaz, who found me gleaning in the field and came to my heart and captured it. I believed that it couldn't be, and he came into my life and made it so. I am his Rib.

My Father

Eugene Yarbrough, the root of my root in Christ. I am wiser because of the love of my Dad. I am blessed to have a walking, tangible image of what a Man, Husband, Grandfather, And a Man of God is and should be. I am honored to be your baby girl.

In Loving Memory Of

Robbie Yarbrough & Gloria Yarbrough

My mothers.

To my Lord & Savior, Jesus Christ - *thank you.*

To every woman who has experienced the darkness and shame of sex-trafficking, I want you to know that I see you. God sees you, and your Exodus is near.

Thank you to my team at Fresh Start Learning, Inc.

Thank you, T.A.L.K. Consulting, for pushing me to the limit.

I thank God for each person who has impacted my journey.

Thank you for celebrating my Exodus and my New Beginning.

-Love Always, Nancy

The Journey

Foreword

Writing a book is not easy — especially when you write one that requires you to express the painful parts of your journey. The parts you'd rather forget, never tell, and pretend they didn't exist. As a survivor of complex trauma, I live my life poured out as a wounded healer. I know that true transformation only takes place in the presence of another soul that is willing to be truly transparent. What you refuse to reveal, you cannot invite God to heal.

One of the things I love about Nancy is her fierce boldness to go into the darkness and become a beacon of light for others. She is an example of how perfect love casts out fear. If you've ever heard her speak, you know the passion she conveys draws you closer to the God she proclaims. You sense His heart, you feel His love, and you are overcome with His presence in her presence.

The Exodus isn't pretty. I'll be honest with you; some parts will take your breath away. Walking with her through this journey was hard work, and some of it *is hard reading* – but it is life-changing. It invites you into truths that some will never tell and inspires you to chase after a God that was in constant pursuit of Nancy's heart throughout her journey.

She thanked me for being her publisher, and I thank her for trusting me with her journey. When someone invites you into their heart, to sit with them in their pain, and to create a narrative to share with the world - that is priceless. I've published several books, this one, however - pulled at the core of my heartstrings. Nancy - I love you, I am proud of you, and I celebrate your Exodus with you.

JoLanda Rogers
Healing Counselor
CEO - T.A.L.K. Consulting, LLC
talkconsulting.net

From The Author

I am the Lord thy God, which have brought thee out of the land of Egypt, out of the house of bondage.
– Exodus 20:2 (NKJV)

The Exodus – Where New Beginnings Happen, is the first of many books I hope to share with the world to create awareness that there is redemption after captivity in sex-trafficking. I have termed my redemption, *The Exodus.* Exodus is the 2nd book of the Old Testament in the Bible, and it shares how God brought the Israelites out of captivity. God can be seen delivering all throughout the Scriptures, but what stands out to me about this particular deliverance is that the Israelites were His chosen people. They were living a life He had not designed for them, and He took it personally to bring them out of slavery and into abundance. Guided by His servant Moses they were promised a land called Canaan as a repayment for their captivity and a reward for their devotion to God.

I want to encourage you to read the book of Exodus to learn more about the experience God's chosen people had battling the reality of the captivity and the struggle of coming out. They were not perfect, but they were loved by the almighty God. Much like me, they continued to make mistakes, and He continued to love them.

In their Exodus, the children of Israel make a covenant with God, and they go on to serve Him as His people and honoring Him as their God. The Exodus for the children of Israel did not happen overnight. Their captors did not want to let them go, and once they were released into freedom, some of them wanted to go back. So much of my life mirrors their struggle of cycles and the everlasting love of God.

As you read this book, I will offer my heart at the opening of each chapter by sharing the message I pray you will receive as you read. Next, you will see moments of reflection – what I call *distant memories,* as I share details of my journey from childhood until now. I want to alert you that some of the things I experienced may create triggers if you have been a victim of sex-trafficking or other forms of abuse and trauma.

If you are triggered, I want to encourage you to pray to God, tell Him how you feel, and invite Him to help you. Some of the things I share in this book I forgot about. However, as my writing process started, they kept coming up, and I knew the purpose was for me to include it in this book. I processed my pain to share a story of healing with you.

After I share my journey, in each chapter, I include a very dear part of the book called *Real Stories from Real Survivors*. I've been blessed to work with so many women and hold their hand into their Exodus. Some of the women I've worked with have elected to share their journeys with you as well. If you read something that stands out to you, breaks your heart, or perhaps, even makes you angry – can I ask you to pray? Pray for the story you are reading, pray for the woman behind the story. Pray for those who were impacted by their pain and pray for me as I pray for you.

Hopefully, you have also purchased a copy of the accompanying companion journal. If you have not, I want to encourage you to purchase the journal as well. For some of the things you read, you will need a safe place to process, and I believe the journal will allow you to do that. Thank you for walking with me, I pray that whoever you are and wherever you are, your life will be blessed.

-Nancy Yarbrough-Banks

Do you have your Companion Journal?

Here are some ideas to get the most out of my journey:

- Invite a small group together and read through the book using the companion journal as a talking guide.
-Host a book club, read the book, and come together once you are done to discuss how this book transforms your life.
-Contact me for a one on one talk-back on the journey to my *Exodus*.
-Invite me as a guest reader to your next advocacy or empowerment group.

The *Genesis* of it All

The bible begins with *Genesis* as its first book and talks about a great big God that had great big plans for the earth that was unformed, uninhibited, and a blank canvas for the ultimate Creator. One thing I love about the book of *Genesis* is that God had a plan in mind from the very beginning. He knew his intended purpose of everything, and He planned for it all to be good.

Genesis is the beginning. As your eyes skim the pages of my heart, I want you to know that your starting point begins wherever you are willing to start. How far back will you go to experience the healing you need to experience? For me to fully celebrate my *Exodus*, I had to go back to the beginning. The very beginning of everything I could remember. I needed to look at how I got here, what was going on when I was born to my mom and my dad, and how those things impacted me.

Not everyone is willing to go back this far; for some, going back is painful. If you are brave enough to go back, then in every place you found pain, you can also find healing. I know this because I was willing to take this journey back - back to the beginning. So your *Genesis* can start where you want it to start. What part of your life are you willing to dive into? What part are you ready to explore? I know some purchased this book because they've heard me speak, and they've listened to the triumph. Not all have heard the trauma. Are you ready to receive the details of my journey? The details aren't pretty. I want there to be a stirring in your heart. I want you to know that there are some things I cried over as I poured the words of my life onto these pages. But I poured them out for you.

I poured them out for the woman, and for the man, that doesn't know where to begin to express their *Genesis*.

I'll be honest; I didn't know where to start. I thought, do I tell them about the trauma of my parents' divorce and how this changed my life, or about my first experience of sex being rape? What about the corruption of my sexuality because of sexual abuse? Do I tell them about how quickly drugs took over my life and kept me in a cycle for decades? Where do I start? Where will you start? For me, I'm glad that I'm comfortable starting at any place in my story because each moment is now revealed to me as good, and I understand God had intentions of His design and purpose to lead me to an *Exodus.*

Each moment where I saw death, He saw life. Each moment I wanted to give up; He knew the outcome would be my *Exodus,* and giving up was not an option. There were times throughout my journey I *tried* to die and could not. God knew at my *Genesis,* at my beginning, that His plans for me were to bring Him glory. So with that, there is no part of my story that I am afraid to tell. No part of my story that I am ashamed to tell, and no part of my story that I will not tell – especially if it will bring healing to those that need it. You see, I know this book will be read by those that are interested in knowing my story - those that want to know how I went from the street to a TEDx Talk or how I went from the gutter to become a business owner and community advocate.

I also know there will be those that hold this book that have not yet seen their *Exodus,* they struggle with their *Genesis,* and for some, this book will be the turning point that transforms their life. This book will be the pivotal moment, like in the bible, when Moses was sent to deliver Israel. If you are that person and you are stuck in a journey that you desperately long to come out of, I need you to know even before you begin reading my life story that your *Exodus* is here. This is mine, and

I'm taking you back, as far back as I can remember – to the *Genesis* of it all.

Distant Memories…

If you asked me to tell you about my life, about my *Exodus*, it wouldn't be complete unless I started at the beginning. My *Genesis,* if you will. I was born into a two-parent home at 235 East Chambers Street in Milwaukee, Wisconsin, and I am the youngest of four children. We lived in what you would call duplex housing. We lived at the bottom, and my parents rented out the top. Although the technical term is we lived in the downstairs unit, while my parents rented the upstairs unit – in so many ways, my experiences in this house represented the bottom, and I craved a different experience of life living at the top.

I remember there were always loud noises that children could not be a part of because these noises happened after our bedtime. My mom was a gambler, and she gambled almost anything. Our house was often full of men and women coming to sit at the card table, and money was always involved. I would try to sneak out to watch what was going on, and my uncle would sit me on his lap before I was reminded to stay out of *grown people stuff* and go back to bed. The aroma was the smell of liquor and cigarette smoke, and so that to me was grown people stuff. They would laugh and make jokes, and so the idea of *grown people stuff* wasn't such a bad idea to me. I liked it.

Christmas was a big deal in our house, we would always have a small Christmas tree put up, and there would be nothing under the tree until the morning of Christmas. Literally, **nothing**. We had a skinny tree, and it would look so weird standing over in the corner and then waking up Christmas morning, and suddenly, the tree would be FULL of gifts, toys, and games! The journey to my *Exodus* has been somewhat like an empty Christmas tree. Knowing that joy is coming, that deliverance is near, and anxiously awaiting its arrival until one day it finally arrives, and it is full of everything I could have ever imagined or desired.

Being born into a two-parent home really does make a difference. While my mother struggled with gambling, my father was a present force in our home. He was always telling us what we shouldn't be doing and giving us instructions to keep us safe. He would have conversations with us over dinner about our day. I remember playing a game where we would put sticks in the water to race and watch to see which one of us had the fastest floating stick. The way my father called my name mattered to me. When I heard Nancy Marie… I knew I was in trouble. He always told us not to play in the street, and I remember one night I was being chased, and I ran out into the street, and the entire block could hear *"Nancy Marie!!!"* and I knew it was my father calling me. He was standing 6"2' and looking out the doorway right at me. There were other moments he would call my name with an endearing tone that spoke with authority and also affirmation.

In the early years of my life, I wanted for nothing. We had new clothes, toys to play with, and I had an imagination that could take me all across the world even though we lived at the bottom. One time I remember my brother and I created a secret world that we could escape too. If you create a secret world, you need a door to get there, right? Of course, you do. So my brother and I drew a large purple door on one of the walls in our house. To us it seemed like a good idea, our parents did not think so, but because we were the youngest, our older sister also got in trouble. That was consistent in my early years; if one was in trouble, we all were in trouble.

This is so important to me because our parents were teaching us responsibility for each other. If one was in trouble, then you go get them; you make sure you are there for them, so they don't get in trouble in the first place. When a person goes through the things that I went through, the most important thing you need is family. You need somebody that will love you anyway and love you unconditionally. The painful part is that so many people who end up living the life I did, that's the one thing we do not have in our lives - and that's family. It makes it easier for other people to hurt us and abuse us because no one is there for us.

5,6,7,8, those were the best years of my life. I remember picking the plums off of a tree in our yard and eating so many plums my stomach would hurt. We had such a big back yard, and then the people next to us had an apple tree, and there was always fruit to eat and always a place to play. There was a part of my life, in the early years that I felt so free, I loved being me, and there are countless memories I reflect on that I know I was truly loved.

But the other side of my *Genesis* was traumatic for me. I was teased for having big lips, not so long hair. My sister would beat people up for talking about me; she protected me. She stood up for me in the way I would later experience God standing up for me. It didn't matter who came against me; she stood up and fought for me. She fought her best friend for me, her boyfriend for me. She would fight the entire world for me. Even in all her fighting for me, it could not erase the deep pain I experienced each time she had to fight. She was fighting for a reason. She was fighting because I was bullied, friendless, and afraid.

My sister was eight years older than me, and she meant everything to me, growing up. The people that would pick on me and tease me were often older than me, they were her age, and she always took care of it for me. When you are a child and not understanding why people are talking about you and being mean to you, it leaves a devastating impact. I know that as I moved through my journey this deep pain gave access for me to surrender to more pain caused by *the life*style I would fall into. I had such a loving and warm heart and these girls and even boys would be so mean to me. It was mostly all of the black kids, and even though my clothes were nice, my hair wasn't long enough to wear the beads the other girls could wear. We attended an inner-city school, but we didn't have an inner-city life. We had both parents, cute clothes, and our parents owned our home. Those were differences from the other kids around us that made us stand out.

My mom gambled so much that my sister raised me. I remember her trying hard to pull the little hair I had together and make me feel beautiful. Her voice of love was something I carried with me, and it meant the world to me. She taught me how to catch the bus and how to get around town. Everywhere we went, she would tell me the street names and where we were and how to get back home. I don't know where I would be without my sister; I know I keep saying it, but she *really meant the world to me.* She was my protector and my best friend, but she could not be the mother I needed.

My life changed when my sister got her *own* life. She had less time for me. When I lost the presence of my sister always being around, me laying my head in her lap and her braiding my hair, I was lost. It was during this same time that my two-parent home became a one-parent home because my parents divorced. I didn't even know things were going wrong between them.

One day they told me I was going to visit my grandparents and put me on a Delta flight to see them. I remember flying by myself as a child and the fear of being alone. The aloneness gripped me. I figured if I could make it through the plane ride and see my grandparents, see a familiar face, I would be okay. When I got off the plane, I didn't see my grandparents. I was in an unfamiliar environment with unfamiliar people, and I had no idea what was going on. This is a scenario I would find myself in often while on the journey to my *Exodus.*

Eventually, my grandparents showed up and took me home with them. After my visit with them, I returned home, and when I did – my dad was gone. There was no explanation about what happened. I was use to having my dad in the house.

Use to having a family that was somewhat intact, and suddenly that was gone. That lower unit became the bottom for me.

I was daddy's little girl (I still am). His absence left me uncovered. Not only was he gone. My sister was also gone, which left me as *free game* for whoever wanted to do whatever to me. My brother quickly became my bully instead of my protector. I remember so many moments waiting for my mom to come and pick me up. To be the protector, my sister was, to be the presence my father was, but she was not. One event for school, I watched the door for her to come, I imagined that maybe even my dad would walk through the door, but neither of them came. Every parent walked in but mine. I cried so hard waiting for my mom, and when I was picked up after the event, there was no conversation about it. No one said anything. At that moment I learned my tears weren't worth being responded too.

Remember the gambling I mentioned? Well, it got worse. My mom didn't have the patience my sister had with my hair, so she would put a hat on my head that had hair sowed around the hat and made me wear it. Imagine a little girl with a hat on - that had a *wig* attached to it. She was so consumed by gambling, and all of the things she had going on, she didn't have time for me. There were days I would spend hours after school at a racetrack, bowling alley, wherever she had to be to feed her gambling habit. I would sit there and watch. Those moments of connection between mother and daughter did not exist. Girls need a connection with their mom. I didn't want for material things, but I craved a maternal presence. Our life was completely different when my dad was gone.

Rebellion kicked in around 10 or 11 when my dad got a new girlfriend. She had children of her own, and I remember my dad introducing them to me, and my entire mind was instantly cluttered with questions. Why do they have *my* dad? He wanted me to get to know her children, but as a child, all I could think of is; this woman and her children have stolen my dad. It was during this time in my life so much more would be stolen from me. I didn't take robbery lightly. At least not at first. I remember watching her walk outside and running to the upstairs bedroom to lean my head out the window and spit on top of her head. I expected her to kill me. At least beat me. Maybe hate me enough to give my dad back. She did not. She took the time to talk to me and told me that she wasn't trying to steal my dad. She reminded me he was my dad (*I knew that already*) – but she said to me "I don't want to take him from you, he's yours, and I want to be yours as well." As sweet as that sounded, as a child I could not understand the words that came out her mouth. I was just thankful to be alive after spitting on a grown woman's head.

Once my dad was out of our home, the molestation started. It seemed like there was a mark on my head that said *now available*. I can't name all of my abusers, and I'm not even sure if the names matter. I know that there were many; family, friends, friends of the family, whoever. This abuse awakened sexual feelings in me. I didn't know how to control it, and so I struggled with involuntary masturbation. I was constantly touching myself because once those experiences started, and I liked some of them, I had to have more of them. Masturbation for children is not exploration, especially when it is triggered because of abuse. It is a direct response to something invasive that has happened to a child and introduced them to a world of feelings they can't control. When the pleasure sensations take over, a child can't delay gratification; they seek to satisfy.

After a while, I not only wanted to experience it, but I wanted to tell someone else to do it, so I started allowing abuse to happen. I would promise not to tell if the older boys touched me, I would tell them to do it just a little so that we wouldn't get in trouble. This was the *Genesis* of my learning to manipulate abuse to make me feel in control. Around 12, I started liking boys, and I was what they called a *fast-tail* girl. My hair eventually started to grow, and I was able to do something to make myself look somewhat attractive. What my beauty could not attract, I learned that my sexuality could – *and it did.*

*   *   *   *

Everyone has a beginning. There is a reason you act the way you do, the reason you feel fear at awkward moments, a reason you crave affection in ways that you *should not.* A reason you crave affection in ways you wish you *would not.* I wish I knew how much my *Genesis* laid the foundation for what I would experience later in life. I would have given myself more grace. I would have sought help sooner. I would have loved myself enough not to blame myself for some of the choices I made. I am glad I know now.

Thoughts From The Biblical Exodus…

Before the children of Israel got to the point of being enslaved, they multiplied. *Exodus* 1:7 (NKJV) talks about how they were fruitful and how they increased significantly, they were taking over, and those in the land were afraid of what they could become. There was greatness among them and greatness within them. I think for many that find themselves in captivity to sex trafficking and other forms of abuse and trauma - we, like the children of Israel belong to God, and He put great things in us from the beginning. People can often see our greatness even when we can't, and it scares them.

I'll highlight some of the parallels that I feel blessed me as God delivered me out of a horrific lifestyle. Remember, I want you to read through the book of *Exodus* because as I take you on this journey, I'll share with you how my life experienced an *Exodus* that caused new beginnings to happen.

Those in authority were so afraid of what the Israelites would become that they conspired in Exodus 1:10 to deal *shrewdly* with them – and have a strategy so that if war broke out, they would not rise and win. I understand their fear because I look back on so many experiences when those that held me captive were afraid too. They didn't say it, but I could sense they knew if I discovered how much God loved me, how much He was willing to fight for me, they could no longer control me. I didn't know it then, but I now know how powerful I was from the beginning. The goal was to hold the children of Israel in captivity, cause divisions among them, work them until exhaustion and break them down until they believed that there was no help for them in God.

God had a plan for you before you were created. His plans for you were good, just like His plans for me were good. His plans don't change. Even when life happens and things come to challenge our faith, even if we make bad decisions or if we end up at the bottom – He still has a good plan. He had this plan at the *Genesis* of it all.

Real Stories From Real Survivors...

My Exodus came unexpectedly. One way my abuser kept me trapped is that he told me if I left, he would kill my mom. Well, my mom died. As painful as that was, her death was my freedom. I left the day he broke my nose, and I heard something in my spirit say act like you're falling out, which I did. He jumped out of the car, and when he did, and I could no longer see him, I got out and ran too. I realized I could no longer take my children through this traumatic life. I am a survivor because of God's grace and mercy. He had another plan for my life in which I live today. I teach other women a new way to live, and I spread the love and the word of God. I teach myself as well as others how to apply His word to their lives one second, one minute, and one hour at a time. Showing up everyday living free. No longer trapped inside my emotions, I was a prisoner of my mind until my Exodus.

V.C.

The Exodus

*B*rokenness

One of the reasons I started with my *Genesis* is because my *Genesis* created my brokenness. If you are brave enough to look at things that happened in your childhood, you can begin to connect the dots to things that happened in your adolescence, your young adult life, and even now as you're an adult. The *Genesis* of a thing matters; it matters that we understand our *Genesis,* according to God, was destined to be good. He had a plan and has a plan for each of us.

Sometimes I look back over my life and think about all the people that were affected by my brokenness. I was affected by the brokenness of others, but I can only take responsibility for mine. Sometimes we don't realize how others can suffer by the mess in our lives. They become broken because our broken pieces cut into their lives. I think about the countless sleepless nights my father must have had wondering where I was and what was happening to me.

The brokenness that I caused to my children by having them placed in foster care, stealing from mom to feed my addiction. I missed so much of my children's lives because I was so broken. I wasn't there to help them ride their bike, and I wasn't there for the first day of school. Years and years have gone by, and I can still see the result of some of my brokenness in their lives. I thank God for how He is healing their lives and making them great men and women. They watched me crash and burn so many times, and as they experience things in their life, I can understand how their *Genesis* has impacted them. I can also point them to God to restore them in areas I hurt them, but I don't have the power to heal them.

When it comes to brokenness, I have to wonder, what is your breaking point? I believed for a while that I couldn't be broken. I thought I was superwoman. My heart was so hard; I could not feel even to know how broken I was. When God allowed me to feel again, it was like a dam broke through, and the flood of tears that I held in for years begin to overflow. Brokenness before Him is not a bad thing; if you don't allow the breaking process to happen, you can't heal properly. You have to feel to heal. Over the last decade or more, I've been invited to speak on platforms I know for sure I do not deserve. Before I go out, I rush to find a bathroom and break before the Lord. I cry out to Him and invite Him into every thought that I have. I allow Him to strip away any negative thinking that would come in my mind.

Being broken before God allowed me to face the memories of all the things I've done, the positions I put myself in, and the mistakes I've made. It also allowed me to give Him the things I had no control over, the things that I didn't deserve, and the times I was unprotected. After I was broken, genuinely broken before Him, He was able to rebuild me. As He is restoring me, I can offer up to Him the pain from those I've broken in the process.

Distant Memories…

My cousin was such a big part of my life. The way I saw it, she was much prettier than I was, her hair was longer – and long hair was everything to me. We were more than cousins; we were like sisters. I wanted another sister so bad because my sister, who meant the world to me, was living a life of her own. A life she deserved to live; it just left my life with a void that could not be filled. My cousin filled this void the best she could, and she was now my sister.

I went to Hamilton high school, and started entertaining boys, and people started paying more attention to me. I liked the attention. It was like my cousin, and I had a secret communication. We stuck together. Even when we hung out with boys, we looked out for each other. We would go over a boy's house, and each of us would have a boyfriend, and we allow them to touch us and us touch them, but the rule was – *no sex*. We would check in with each other to make sure we were both *good*, and we would be on to our next adventure. I liked the attention.

The beginning of high school was a great time for me. There were skating nights in the city, and we would go skating all night. Even when my mom told me I couldn't go hang out, I'd go anyway. When she would try to discipline me, I'd laugh. I was enjoying *the life* of a typical rebellious teenager. But much of my rebellion was rooted in the unexpressed pain of my childhood, the longing for my dad, the need for my mom, and the consequences of uncontrolled sexuality awakened by early sexual abuse.

My life changed the day one of my attempts to be in control of a sexual experience became out of my control. I dated an older boy in high school, but even with older guys, I knew the routine – and I expected them to know too. This guy came too close to having sex with me, and I was terrified. I was in a compromised position, and I could not control the outcome. At this moment, the fear I felt the first time I was abused came back. That feeling of being out of control. I couldn't acknowledge it at the time, but I now realize that all those years, I never was in control. I was playing on dangerous ground, and it was catching up with me. It was another girl and me at a house with our boyfriends, and I could hear her struggling, and from the sounds, I knew she had been raped. Her struggle scared me, and so I decided not to struggle. I think my lack of struggle saved me. At least it saved me this time. The next time, I would not be so lucky.

*   *   *   *

You know the feeling you get in your gut that tells you not to do something? I had this feeling on the day my cousin and I were approached by a group of older guys. We knew them from around the block, and so we convinced ourselves that it was okay to talk to them even though we *really didn't* know them at all. We were walking home, and they pulled over and asked us did we want a ride. My gut said no, but our youth and ignorance said yes. My cousin told me that we would be fine and not to be scared. I trusted her. I never trusted myself. I didn't feel like I could be trusted, but for some reason, I felt like she could.

We got in the car, and I remember at the time we lived on 35th and Garfield. I was good at navigating my way around the city because my big sister taught me how to catch the bus when I was a little girl. She would point out the major street names to me and tell me which roads would lead to home. As they drove, I quickly realized that the roads they were taking would not lead us home. They made a left when they should have made a right. I spoke up as where we were going, but fear had already gripped me. They said they needed to check on something before taking us home. We ended up turning into an abandoned building that is currently near the city's social service and welfare building. To this day, I view that side of town differently.

Once near the building, they told us to get out, my cousin and I had whispered to ourselves that as soon as we got out of the car, we would run, and we did. We both knew by this time something wasn't right. They jumped out the car behind us, and as we ran I was ahead of my cousin, she had asthma, and one of them caught up with her. I turned around and went back voluntarily because we had a code, never leave each other behind - *so I thought.*

As we walked up the stairs to this building and into an apartment, they were hitting us in our heads and calling us stupid for trying to run. I closed my eyes as the slaps went across my face and my head. When I opened my eyes, I noticed at least 4 to 5 guys that were in this apartment, and they were there waiting on us (it felt like the room was full of men). I couldn't even imagine what was going to happen to us. I would soon find out. One of them pulled me into a room, and my cousin said she had to go to the bathroom. I wish I would have been smart enough to think of that. While in the room, I heard one of the guys yell *"that bitch is gone, she jumped out the window."* She jumped out the window to her freedom and left me. I was terrified. My cousin, my partner -was **gone**. I was alone in an apartment bedroom with a man I did not know, and there were several men waiting to run a train on me. I was 13 or 14.

I nearly blacked out from the fear and wished I had fully succumbed to the blackout so I would have no memories of what happened - but fate was not that kind to me. I remember everything. I remember the pain and the force of entry; I remember my thoughts racing. I remember holding my breath. I remember wondering where my dad was. Out of all the things to think of, I thought of my dad. I thought of him because I knew if he was here, there is no way any of this would have happened to me. I was unprotected.

After the rape, he realized the trauma done to my body and called it my period. I didn't care. I was glad he saw his damage. I was glad he knew my pain. He yelled and told the other guys, *"this nasty bitch on her period."* I'd never heard the b-word used so much, but it would soon become a regular term used to describe me as I journeyed to my *Exodus*. Thankful for some sense of humanity and decency they threw a towel at me to clean myself up. I promised them that if they took me home, I wouldn't tell. I just wanted to get out, to go home, to be safe again.

My cousin made it to the house and told our family I had gotten into a car with some guys, and they kept me and that she didn't know where I was. We were only separated, maybe 45 minutes, but to me, it felt like an eternity. I didn't want them to know which house I lived in, so I told them to drop me off a few blocks away. This would give me time to come up with a story just in case I needed one. By the time I made it to the house and walked through the door, my dad had already been called, he was already there waiting on me and had his shotgun ready.

As much as I wanted to run into his arms and tell him what happened, I couldn't. I was ashamed, I was in pain, and I knew if he knew, that he would be so disappointed in me. I could not disappoint him. I learned to face trauma with a lie. I made up a story that was good enough to believe. I told them that after my cousin got away, I waited until the guys started talking to each other, and I ran and got away too. They asked me did anything happened to me. I told them no. But so much had happened to me. Far beyond the experience was the imprint it left on my soul, the familiar place it would become for me, and the shame it left with me. My aunt decided it was not a good idea for my cousin and me to hang out as much as we did. I agreed.

My cousin and I never talked about why she left me. Why she ran, even after I came back for her, I could have kept running, but I didn't. I went back for her. I would see times throughout my journey where God put people in my life to come back for me. My going back was not in vain. My dad decided at that moment that I was coming to live with him.

*   *   *   *

I went to live with my dad, and at this time, my dad had remarried, and there were other children there. Although I had met them before, it was a completely different experience living with them. I had to move schools and became the only person in my dad's house that felt like they didn't fit in. My stepmom had a daughter, and she became my baby sister. I finally had someone around that was younger than I was. My stepmom tried so hard to build a relationship with me. I made it almost impossible. It was one of the most challenging times in my life. I never rebounded from what happened. I started to lie about everything. Trust was broken, and now fear consumed me. I would always write letters to my mom and dad, apologizing for being the type of daughter I was and pledging to be better. I never felt that I was better; I kept messing up.

Sexual abuse became known to me again, this time, I didn't care. I was stiff, numb, immune to it all.

Thoughts From The Biblical Exodus...

While in captivity, the children of Israel were broken. In Exodus 2:24-25 (NKJV) it mentions that God heard their groaning and he remembered his covenant with Abraham, with Isaac, and with Jacob, so He looked on them and was concerned about them. Even when there are times we may not feel it or even believe it, God hears our groaning. He is concerned about us. It could be a situation that you feel you placed yourself in; maybe you were disobedient as a child or made poor choices as an adult. That doesn't matter, God will still hear you, and He will still rescue you.

I know it is a different perspective to consider, but that day in the apartment, I feel like God heard my groaning. He intervened and saved me from something that could have been far worse; it could have been deadly. I thank God that so many times in my life He heard me, and He was concerned about me. He is a good, good, God. If I can look at the terrible situation that happened in my life as a teenager, I want you to be encouraged to look at situations in your life through a God lens as well. Yes, I know it was evil, I believe that even in evil situations, God is aware of it and yes, He is concerned about us.

There was an evil situation that happened in the book of Exodus. Think about the declaration from Pharaoh that all the male children of the Hebrew women should die. He was so afraid of the power that the Hebrew boys would have in strengthening their people that he called to have them assassinated immediately at birth. Even with this happening,

God was doing something good. He was preparing a deliverer by the name of Moses that would be spared and would lead the children of Israel into their Exodus. The Levite woman that gave birth to Moses wanted her son to live and be spared. She even understood that sparing him could mean sending him down the Nile river, and she did – only for him to be saved ultimately by God.

Pharaoh's daughter saw Moses in the basket on the river and felt bad for him; she had mercy on him. God will always have a plan to place someone around you that will feel your pain, and just as Pharaoh's daughter did for Moses, they will see you drifting along the water and draw you out. If help has not come in your life, I need you to know and to believe that help **is** coming.

Real Stories from Real Survivors

I remember feeling so small and lonely and misunderstood. The energy from those feelings is exactly what attracted my perpetrator. As he shaped me into his personal slave, I remember being consumed by the feelings of embarrassment and disgust. It was the nasty looks that I received and the hurtful names that I was called by the people I loved and trusted that made me cry out to God. I cried, I prayed, and He heard me. I never wanted anyone to feel as small as I did. I am committed to building people up in my community, and I am now a voice for the voiceless.

R.M.

The Promise

I think of the promises that people made to me and never kept. The promises I made to myself and didn't hold. The promise that life could get better, but I never believed that it could. As you're reading my *Exodus*, do you have outstanding promises to yourself? Are there things you told yourself you would change, things you would do better, and things you would seek help for? Are you keeping those promises? I would feel so lost when people would make promises to me, but then I was challenged to look at the greater damage being done when I did not keep the promises that I made to myself.

What I learned about promises is just like God gave a promise to the children of Israel to deliver them and bring them out; He had the same promise and hope for me. To keep me and bring me out. I could not even understand that as truth during the dark moments of my journey. I thought for sure that God had forgotten about me, that He wasn't thinking of me, and that there is no way He would come and get me from the pit of hell I jumped into - but He did.

Promises are to be kept, not just to be made, and you have to learn how to keep the promises that you make to yourself. If there is anything that I want you to take away from this part of my journey is a promise to heal. A commitment to do the work you need to do and allow God to heal your life. I know that He can and that He will. I have full confidence in Him *for* you that He will keep His word. He will do whatever it takes to bring you out. Will you allow Him? Even when I didn't acknowledge God throughout my journey, He would send specific experiences, and people along the way to lead me to my *Exodus*, but I wasn't ready to go. I couldn't see that was their purpose.

You can't rely on other people to fulfill the promises you make to yourself. Think about something so simple as a promise you make in the new year. Do you keep those promises? Did you know that when you break a promise to yourself, you also break a promise to everyone else around you? People are connected to your promise. I didn't realize this until I fully accepted the promise that God had for me. The promise that He would never leave me nor forsake me, the promise that He would be with me always. The promise that He had a plan for my life. The promises were there; for years, I couldn't see them, feel them, or receive them. I can now.

* * * *

Distant Memories…

The next part of my transition was being made to go live with my dad because I had gotten out of control. Living with my dad and his new family was stressful. I had to go to a new school, learn a new way of doing things, it was a lot, and again, no one talked about it. Decisions were just made, and things happened. When changes happen for a child or teenager, adults need to talk to them and tell them what's going on. I was trying to fit in and get use to how they did things, and it was so hard. So much went on in that house. A house I was supposed to become stable in, but I could not because I experienced the same things all over again from being a kid - unwanted touches and no one to tell.

* * * *

My first boyfriend was a guy named Joe, and because of the rape, I was ready and willing to be with him because that's what

I had to offer. It was different for me because that's not what he wanted. He really liked me, but I didn't know how to be *really liked.* Eventually, he liked me enough for sex, so that's what we did. I found an escape in marijuana early in my teenage years and used alcohol as a way to numb the pain I felt but couldn't tell anybody about. Forming relationships with older men seemed natural to me. It was easier for me to relate to older men because every experience of intimacy was initiated by someone older than me, from being a child and being abused to the rape that happened during my freshman year in high school. Everyone was always older so that was all I knew.

My hair grew, but it was so damaged, my stepmom tried to fix it by putting a jerry curl in it, and it made all of my hair fall out - I went back to being *bald-headed* Nancy. I was so embarrassed. That was the last thing I needed. At a new school with no hair. I found out that short hair wasn't the end of the world because that's when I met my unborn child's father. He was so fine. Light skinned, green eyes, there was no way I thought he would be interested in me, but he was.

Of course, he was older than me, and dating people older than me kept me promiscuous because that's what they were interested in, so that's what I did. I was dating him, and I got pregnant. The reason I call that baby my unborn child is my mom told me I was too young to have a baby and took me to have an abortion. That again was a reminder of having my choices taken away because it wasn't up to me. I remember her taking me to the abortion clinic and how traumatic that event was for me. I felt life leave my body, not just my babies' life, but my life too.

* * * *

By the time I was in the 10th or 11th grade, my stepmom got saved, which made my dad get saved because she said they could not stay together unless he got saved, too - and he did. Saved meant that they accepted the Lord Jesus Christ as their Savior, and they turned their lives around to live a life that was pleasing to Him.

One time my dad was at home by himself in the shower, and he said the Holy Spirit came over him and told him to drink the water, and he did, and the Holy Spirit told him to drink the water again, and he did. After that, the Holy Spirit told him there would be somethings he wouldn't be able to do anymore and somethings he would. God changed his life that day. He spoke in a heavenly language and later accepted his call to ministry.

My dad became a pastor, and he is still a pastor today. It's amazing to look at his life now because I remember the man he was. I remember the drinking, 3-pack a day cigarette smoking man – and I watched God completely change his life. He started taking us to church, we went to every service that was held, and anytime the doors were open – he took us to church. That became my first experience with Christ at Ezekiel Church of God in Christ. That was the first time I felt His presence and knew that He loved me. I still had so many unresolved things happening inside of me, but I could feel the love of Christ. I didn't know why He loved me, but I was convinced He did.

* * * *

In the 11th grade, I went back to live with my mom. I complained to her that I didn't fit in at my dad's house, and I didn't want to be there. They had rules, and I didn't like to follow their rules. I manipulated the situation to go back and live with my mom. It was one of the worst things I ever did because it gave me too much freedom. I didn't like the rules at my dad's house, but I couldn't handle the freedom at my mom's house. Instantly I had time on my hands to feed the things that were in me. I could smoke weed, drink, try drugs, have sex, date older guys, do whatever I wanted to do.

I worked at Taco Bell and Walgreens, and with my older boyfriend also came the introduction of cocaine into my life. The brokenness in that season went from one person introducing me to cocaine, to someone showing me how to *toot* it, to another person introducing me to *smoking* it. When pain is rooted, you will do anything to try and find comfort. All of the pain from my *Genesis* sat in my soul. Here I was, a 16-year-old girl who had an abortion and was now a drug user, and then found out I was pregnant again. This time my baby wouldn't be unborn, I had my first child at 17. I still wasn't ready – but he was *mine*. After having him, I remember getting the AFDC check(aid to families with dependent children) for $440 a month and using that to feed our cocaine habit.

Having a baby didn't slow me down; it wasn't the pivotal moment of change in my life. Things continued to get worse. My boyfriend and I kept getting drugs, he started stealing the money from me to buy more drugs, and although we had moved out together, we got put out for not paying the rent, so I went back home. That was the start of my cocaine addiction.

My addiction is what lured me into *the life* I needed a way to feed my habit, and people my age didn't have cocaine habits, so I needed to hang out with people older than I was. Remember, I was already used to doing this because it had become the story of my life – older people. The problem with hanging out with older people is that it caused people I thought were my friends to sell me out because they knew men who wanted to be with a younger girl, and I was that more youthful girl.

* * * *

My friend's brother wanted to be a pimp, and he wanted me to be one of his girls. At the time, we didn't *call* it that. He was just an older guy that was digging me and happened to be the one holding the bag. He would take me to private parties, truck stops, and the spiral started. Before I knew it - I was too far gone to stop it. Everything happened so fast; I didn't know what was happening, I just knew it *was* happening, and I couldn't stop it. I had access to money when I needed it, access to drugs, and nobody asked how I was getting the money. It was never talked about. I would go in and out of town. They trained me and taught me the ropes, and I learned them quickly. During this time, "pimping" was glamorized at events like the player's ball. Although I was trying to maintain a status, I didn't realize I had become just another drug-addicted hoe. The reality of those words hit my gut like a ton of bricks.

*   *   *   *

Thoughts From The Biblical Exodus...

When it was time for the children of Israel to be released from captivity, God used that same baby boy that was faced with an evil situation to bring out a great nation. Not only was Moses faced with the threat of being murdered from the day of his birth, if you go on to read in Exodus, you will learn that Moses was also a murderer. He was not perfect. I'm so glad that God chooses to use people that are not perfect, that means that He can still use me.

After Moses committed murder, he ran away. His secret was found out. Shame, guilt, and fear provoked him to run. Sometimes we run when our secrets come out. It doesn't matter how far we run or where we run; God can always see us and find us. He's always watching us. When it was time for Moses to be used by God, God appeared to him through the symbol of a burning bush. God told Moses that he saw the things the children of Israel were facing, He knew how much pain they were in, and He was ready to bring deliverance to them.

Moses, knowing who he was, and what he had done, asked God in Exodus 3:11, "Who am I that I should go to Pharaoh and bring the Israelites out of Egypt?" God knew that Moses was concerned about what the Exodus would look like, and He simply responded to Moses by telling him, "I will be with you." You may not have a literal Moses that comes to declare liberty to your captors, but know when God says that you will be delivered, you **will be** delivered, and there is nothing that can stop it.

Moses was still worried about what to say to Pharaoh. Fear can be deadly when the person you have to approach has murderous intentions. Moses asked God, "what do I say when they ask me who sent me?" God responded with, "I Am Who I Am, I Am has sent me to you." Just as simple as that. Exodus chapter 3 will give you the dialogue between Moses and God.

Any time I am afraid or fearful of anything I have to do, I go to this chapter, and I am reminded that it is the "I Am" that is with me. I am often invited to share my journey with people across the country. Some of them are still in *the life*, and some of them have come out. I never know who will be in the room, and it can be scary. But because I know that "I Am" has sent me and is sending me to pull others into an Exodus - I go with no fear. He promised me He would be there, and He keeps His promises.

Real Stories from Real Survivors

I used to hate that I was victimized, that there are people that use the vulnerabilities of others for their own profit. Even worse is the fact that there are some men who purchase people for their own satisfaction and self-enticement. People aren't for sale. I was sold over and over to the highest bidder until one day, the FBI came along, and I was given a second chance. Someone stepped in and cared about me and loved me until I learned to love myself. Then I learned I could share my story of redemption with people across the world; I could prevent sex-trafficking and change our culture. I went from being a victim to wearing my title of "survivor" as a badge of honor. I'm not ashamed. It is possible, hope is possible. My goal now is to spread hope & prevention for generations to come.

E.M.

The Law of Who I Am

When you come into this world, you are given a name, this name and title are put on you, and it is who you are expected to be. My name was Nancy Yarbrough, and I was expected to be that. I had brown eyes, brown hair; my parents had expectations of what they wanted me to become. They had an image of who they saw I would be in life and gave me a name according to what they believed I would become. The law of what they named me was broken when the world tried to name me something else. I had to learn that it didn't matter what I was called, the fact that they named me with a purpose created a law for who Nancy was supposed to be.

Elementary school chipped away at this when I was bullied for having short hair and big lips. That stayed with me and was one of the reasons I would do things to be liked by others. I felt like I wasn't good enough. I wasn't pretty enough. Boys identified me by making comments about my body, saying I was shaped like a white girl with big legs and big breasts, but no butt.

That carried over into my young adulthood when my first trafficker told me everything I wanted to hear. He told me how pretty I was and how he loved the shape of my body and the tricks the *Johns** wanted to do with me because I was just what they wanted. The men that wanted to take advantage of me were also identifying me, but they did so with lies. Lies that benefited them and robbed me.

It wasn't long before other names and titles were given to me that tried to define who I was or who I was supposed to be. I was *Brown Sugar* on the stage, and I was *Live Wire* in the bedroom, and on the street, I was *Kim the Cutter.* People gave me an identity, and it wasn't attached to the law of who I was or who I was supposed to be. The experience of being molested gave me the title of being fast and promiscuous. I never dealt with the trauma of the rape, so when I acted out, I was identified as a liar and hardheaded. The law of who I was became shaped into what other people called me. My identity was no longer my own, nor was it free for me to define - it was now what everyone else said about me.

I became trapped in the law of what others defined me by. That I would never be anything, that because of what I was doing and who I had become, I would always be trapped in *the life*style, that there was no hope for me. When someone gives you an identity, and it is not who you were created to be you begin to lose who you really are. I started to believe the lies that created these laws about me.

When Christ came into my life, He exchanged who I was, and even with the titles that I hold now, I lay them all down just to ask God who I am. To sit with Him and allow Him to define me and restore the intentional laws of my identity. I'm not even who I recognize myself to be because I still know that my identification of myself cannot always be trusted. However, the way God identifies me can always be trusted and believed. Who God says I am, I am. There is no question about it. No one can ever break the law of my identity again because I have embraced what God has said about me.

I wonder do you take the time to ask who does God say you are. Once God secured me in who I am, I now call myself by different names. I'm not hopeless or no good. I am reliable, and I am a good friend, I'm dependable, I'm strong, I keep my word, I'm a good wife. Those are my new identities, and I am what He calls me, and that is **His child**. I am somebody.

**a John is another name for a man who buys a woman for sex.*

Distant Memories...

One night at a truck stop, I was sent in to make some money, and when I got in the truck, the guy told me to go to sleep. I was so tired, and he realized that I had been awake for a few days, and he let me sleep. For some reason, I trusted him. He could have just driven off with me, but he didn't, he let me sleep, and he paid me for what it would have cost him to be with me, and I didn't have to do anything. I felt like that was God's olive branch of love telling me to go home. He was always extending His grace to me, even in the most unconventional ways. I had so much gratitude for that moment of sleep. Cramped up in a semi-truck, it was a few hours of rest that I needed so bad.

When I got back to the hotel in the morning, I was well-rested. I was thankful. I went to our room and took out the money the *John* gave me and put it on the table, which was the usual protocol. I looked for the plate so I could have my morning toot of cocaine, and that's when it happened. The man I thought was my friend and that we were in this together, revealed his true colors as my pimp and he beat me.

I realized that I was not in a relationship with someone that loved or even cared about me, but I was in bondage to a pimp. I never thought that he was using me only to make money until I came back without enough money. I was so excited to tell him what happened. I wanted him to know that this guy let me sleep and that I didn't have to do anything for the money, he just gave me the money, and I brought it home to him.

That wasn't what he wanted to hear. The time I spent sleeping was the time I could have been making money. I learned at that moment that I was working on a quota. This had never been discussed with me, but it never had to be because I always came back with the money. He asked me where the rest of the money was. I didn't know what to say, I was so thankful for the rest, and I expected him to be as well.

The next thing I knew, he was beating me up and telling me I bet not ever come back without what he sent me out to get. Fear immediately kicked in, and I had no idea what I had gotten myself into. The fear of not being loved, not being accepted, not being wanted all came rushing back. It wasn't the fear of him beating me. It was the fear of him not loving me.

After that, he never had to worry about me not meeting the quota. I went above and beyond; I made sure that I would be one of his best girls, and I would do whatever I needed to do to earn his love. I always wanted to be accepted and loved. All of the bullying from elementary school came back to me again. I felt like that same little girl that still wanted to fit in.

Again, the hurtful part was not meeting his quota; it was that I didn't get the love and affection I'd typically get when I came back in. To me, that was love. He treated me like his favorite girl. I looked forward to that. I loved it when he loved me and made me feel special, and I needed that. People don't realize that when you're in captivity, you begin to think that behaviors opposite of love, still feel like love. I was denied his love and denied the plate. He wouldn't give me the toot of cocaine that helped me keep my mind. It helped me stay numb to all of the pain. I didn't get the antidote to help me process what happened the night before or the way he just beat me.

You know, like some people start their morning with coffee and a donut? For me, I started with a drink and a toot of cocaine. This particular morning I didn't get either, and the reality of the pain that ripped through my soul took my breath away.

I thought we were a team, like we had a partnership. I was so deceived and naive about what was happening to me. I *really* believed that we were working together, but I learned that night that I *really* worked for him, and our partnership never existed. That was another moment in my life where I embraced trauma. I embraced it and accepted it as something that I deserved and tried to make a mental note to do better so he would never be disappointed in me again.

I was the same teenager raped and didn't want her father to know because I didn't want him disappointed. I was that same girl touched inappropriately but couldn't tell anybody because I thought it was my fault. I loved it when he loved me; I needed to be loved. People may not realize that in the season of captivity, you don't know that what you are going through isn't normal. Once you become used to it, it seems normal.

*　　*　　*　　*

God continued to step in and provide ways of escape for me. There was a lady named *sugar britches* that groomed me and showed me the ropes; she taught me how to make the most money at the truck stops. A few months later, we were out together to make some money, and after we got done working the stop, she told me to get in her Cadillac and took me to get something to eat. While we were eating she told me she was taking me home because I didn't need to be there. That I didn't belong on the streets or at those stops, that there was more for me. The way she spoke to me made me want to see things differently. She looked beyond *her* pain and captivity to see how she could help set me free.

This woman laid her life on the line for me, the danger of her trying to get me out of *the life* is that women are often made examples of. If my pimp found out that she was trying to get me out, he would have beat her, possibly even killed her. In *the life*, the fear strategy is to send a message to the other girls, to not do the same thing, and try to help another girl. She committed two violations. The first one was to try to get me out, and the second one was to mess with my pimp's money. I wondered if she even knew how dangerous and courageous she was. I've thought about her often and wished that I could find her and thank her for being a representation of God coming to get me here on this earth.

God always left what I call "breadcrumbs of love" for me, and she was one of them. She drove me back to Wisconsin and told me to go home. At that moment, did I stop using drugs immediately? No, but her love for me broke the chain of allowing someone else to use me in that way. I never went back to that pimp. She risked her life for mine. Here is the thing about leaving a pimp; there *really* is no such thing as leaving a pimp. So I knew one day he would come looking for me. I just didn't know what I would do when he did. When I got home I went upstairs to my room, and life almost resumed as usual.

* * * *

Thoughts From The Biblical Exodus...

Moses was worried because of who he was, but he never had to be worried because of who God was. The law and the nature of God were sure to bring Moses victory over Pharaoh. It was an easy win. Not because of Moses, but because of God. God was never afraid of Pharaoh, and I want you to know that God is never afraid of any type of Pharaoh that will arise in your life.

God reminded Moses of who He was. He told him "I am the Lord, the God of your fathers, the God of Abraham, the God of Isaac, and the God of Jacob. This is my name forever, the name by which I am to be remembered from generation to generation." – Exodus 3:15 (NKJV). What makes this verse so powerful is that God tells Moses who I am, and who I will be, will never change. That makes this true for you and me today. God is God.

I am blessed as God reminds Moses that His name will be remembered from generation to generation. I think of my father giving his life to the Lord and creating a change in our generations. I thank God that because of him, it planted a seed in me so that my children and their children can know God – generation to generation.

God also knew that during the time of pursuing freedom that Moses would need the reminder to stand firm and see the deliverance of the Lord. God told Moses that the Lord would fight for him, and he only needed to be still. I know God fought for me so many times I could not fight for myself. He stood between my captors and me and protected me.

He's standing between you and your captors, and He's protecting you too. What I am sharing does not only relate to being delivered from the trafficking lifestyle; it applies to being delivered from anything and everything. God is able.

Moses begin to sing to the Lord in Exodus 15:2-3, he offered up the words "the Lord is my strength and my song; he has become my salvation. He is my God, and I will praise him, my father's God, and I will exalt him. The Lord is a warrior; the Lord is his name." He continues in Exodus 15:11 to say, "Who among the gods is like you, O Lord? Who is like you – majestic in holiness, awesome in glory, working wonders?" Moses could be confident in this declaration of the Lord because he knew the answer was nobody. It was not a question. It was a statement of fact.

I think of drugs, sex, lies, all the things that tried to be like a god to me, that tried to stand between God and me. As my Exodus drew near, I could see more and more that those things did not have more power than the Almighty God. Who is like the Lord? Nobody. I boldly declare that, and I know the law of who He is will save me from who I am whenever I call upon His name.

Real Stories from Real Survivors

I was molested by a family member at the age of 8 until I was 14. I decided to run away because I knew what was going on in our house had to stay in our house, and I could no longer live in that house. I was lured into a trap because I was so hungry, and I really wanted a place to stay. I needed a place to lay my head down, and an older guy came in and asked me was I hungry and bought me something to eat. I was attracted to his looks, and he invited me home with him, and I went. That's when my life changed forever. The first day I was there he told me I belonged to him, he beat me and told me I would make him money. He owned me for three and a half years. I was freed because he was murdered. Although he no longer owned me, the lifestyle was now in me. I continued in the life until one day I was left for dead. That day I knew there was something more in me. I felt that God had something better for me. What gives me strength every day is that I look back on who I used to be, and I talk to countless women who are there now, living that life, and I give them hope. I tell them there is a way out, and I help show them the way.

D.H.

The Cycle

The cycle was one of the most painful parts of my process. It was the hamster wheel. I think about how many times I did things over and over again, repetitively. It was a cycle of constant hurt and constant pain. Men after men. Cycles of loneliness and depression. It was cycles of low self-esteem and self-worth. I could only see myself as I was, I couldn't even imagine seeing anything different. Every time I would come out of *the life*, I would go back in *the life*.

Understanding the cycle of addiction is something not many can do. I would come out, and then I would go back in. It's not that easy to just stop doing drugs and never go back. I was addicted to drugs for many years. I became addicted to crack cocaine and alcohol at the age of 17. I got out at 21, and then I went back at 25, it was constant cycles. Cycles stopped me from fully walking into my *Exodus* because I kept being sucked back into the grip of men, abuse, drugs, all kinds of cycles.

It would be decades before I was sober and drug-free. It wasn't that I couldn't get clean, because I could. It wasn't that I couldn't leave *the life*style because I could do that too. But I kept going back in, each time going deeper and deeper into the darkness that consumed me. I would get jobs, and I would work the job for a while and then I would lose the job, and another cycle would start. Every time the cycle would break, I would go back into the last cycle that was the most familiar. I would ask God to forgive me of my sins, I would confess, I would say I surrender, and then I would go right back in.

I would have "aha" moments where I felt like I could do something different, but different was too scary. After the first few cycles, I could tell that I was losing fragments of myself. They say insanity is doing the same thing over and over and looking for different results but not doing anything different to see them. I had a lot of sobriety and Jesus moments. I would go to God and ask Him what I should do and how can He help me. I cried out. I wanted to be different, but every time I would get out, and life would hit an area of brokenness - I would go back into *the life*style again. I felt so stuck.

Fear gripped me so much. When I tried to do things differently, it was terrifying. Different can be scary when you have been trapped in a cycle for so long. Fear can be so overwhelming that it's easier to do the predictable thing, knowing what is going to happen to you versus not knowing at all. I wanted to change so bad, but I didn't know how to change. When I would try to change, I couldn't because it was so heavy. The weight of all I was doing, all that was happening to me, was too much. What is dangerous about cycles is that the people that keep you connected to them will always be there to pull you back into them. Who you are around, who you allow in your life, those will be the people that determine how long your cycle lasts. I do believe the cliché' that birds of a feather flock together, they really do. They did in my life, which is what kept me in cycles for decades. I WANTED OUT!!!

Distant Memories…

After being home for a short time, I knew this guy who lived across the street from me, and during the time of me leaving and coming back, he had also become hooked on drugs, so now I had a friend that lived close to me that I could do drugs with. It wouldn't be long before my pimp came looking for me. It was snowing outside, and we were upstairs getting high, and my mom was at work. I heard a knock at the door and looked out the window and realized it was him. The fear I felt in my heart that day was enough to send me into a full-blown heart attack. I felt like a little girl again, afraid, and went to hide in the closet. I knew he would come after me, but I was determined never to go back to him.

What he didn't know is that by this time I had a bigger pimp than him, my new pimp was cocaine. I was 20 years old and had been using it for three years. It felt like dog years, years that dragged on forever. Much of it is a blur because I became my *own* renegade. I learned the ropes around the area and made the money I needed to so I could support my habit. I met people who I know to this day are still struggling to get out of *the life*. After a while, I got tired, sick, and tired - I wanted help. I signed myself into a mental health complex and went through a 90-day treatment program where I met my girl's dad. They had a coed treatment facility.

Coed treatment facilities can be a terrible thing because when you are working your program the best you can, that temptation to replace your drug with an unhealthy relationship is almost unavoidable. I replaced my drug with a man that was ten years older than me. Again, I found myself in a relationship with an older man. He eventually got kicked out of the program and told me he had a place for me to stay when I got out. And you better believe that once I got out and finished my program, he was right there waiting for me. I was enjoying his company and developed feelings for him before I realized he relapsed. I didn't know he had an angry side, an abusive side, because I never saw that side when he was clean. When he used his drug of choice, it became just like the pain I'd always known when dealing with men. I knew that I found myself in another place I did not want to be. Instead of going home to a safe place, I went back to what was comfortable; I went back to what I knew. My mom was now raising my son because I was entangled again.

* * * *

Before things got too far, again, God intervened. I went to the army in South Carolina. I was tired again, and I was so tired of being sick and tired, and the military was my way out. It was one of the best decisions of my life. The military provided me with structure, stability, and purpose. All things I needed if I was to see my life change and maintain those changes. No matter how much I tried to change, the spirits of my past, the spirits that I fought to stay away from continued to find me. Once I finished the primary part of the program and went into the technical part of the program, it came with more freedom. We were able to go out to the bowling alley and hang out. I wasn't ready for freedom in that way. I needed to stick with the structure. I thought I could handle having a drink. That maybe I could control my cravings and limit it to alcohol only, but I could not. Once I had that first drink, I needed to have the drugs to go with it. The cycle began again.

It was the grace of God again that stepped in and constrained me before I went too far out. I pulled myself together enough to focus and to finish my program in the army. The next six months were different. I was focused, and it looked like I would make it - like I could *really* make a change and keep it. Both of my parents were writing me letters and caring about me. This was the best part of all of it. Knowing they were thinking of me, and they loved me. I needed to be cared for and loved. I needed them to be proud of me, and for this moment in time they were. Once I completed the program, it was time to go home.

I called home to talk to the love I left and to tell him all the things that happened while I was away. I thought for sure I could come back and help him, as well as myself, to do better and be better. When I called, I heard another girl in the background. The sound of her voice broke my heart, again I was unwanted, unloved, and there was someone more desirable than I was.

I needed to be with him again. I needed to know that he loved me and that he would pick me over her. So when I returned home from the army, I went back to him. The first day I returned home, he had a party, and he planned to get me high again, and it worked. After a year of being back, I was honorably discharged from the army because I was pregnant with my first baby girl. My son was six years old at this time, and from the time of my son until my daughter, I had stints of sobriety. There was a moment I was focused enough to earn a degree in early childhood education. I stayed clean for about four or five years. The military was so good for me; it helped my mind to be organized. It gave me structure and a reason to want to be better.

* * * *

A few years passed, my life continued to have peaks and valleys. I still hadn't dealt with any of the pain of my Genesis or my brokenness and so there continued to be seasons when I struggled with sobriety. Soon after, I met what I thought was the love of my life, my son's dad. I didn't even know I was pregnant by him; I just knew I had enjoyed him, his presence, and the man that he was. He was different. Although we met using drugs, he had such a good heart; his character was genuine. Not all people that use drugs are terrible. Many of them are not – it's the things that drugs cause them to do that makes them seem terrible, but it's not the person.

He was like a superhero in my life. He was a real captain *save a hoe*. I thought he was just like all of the other guys. I offered him some drugs one night, and he declined saying he kept his on the low, I didn't understand what that meant, but I later learned that meant he was a heroin addict, not cocaine. I remember all of us hanging out, and he said that he would be back. I never thought anything of him leaving or if he would *actually* return because, in my mind, he was like every other man.

* * * *

Thoughts From The Biblical Exodus…

I shared how even in my captivity, God would send invitations of freedom. Like the guy in the semi-truck, or *sweet britches.* Even my time of escape by going to the military, God was always guiding me to an Exodus. The children of Israel, once they were guided away from the hands of the Egyptians, they longed for what they once had. They were not satisfied with where they were, and fear of what was to come antagonized them continuously.

I know it may seem hard to understand, but when you are captive for so long, and God gives you freedom when He brings you out – you also have to allow Him to bring your mind out, so you don't think the same and crave the same things. When they complained about food, God gave them bread from heaven.

There were even moments where they refused to obey the commandments of the Lord. The Lord allowed them to experience the consequences of their behavior, but He never changed how He felt about them. Yes, He gave them consequences. But He never said, "I hate you; you're no good." He didn't tell them, because you keep messing up, I'm going to send you back to captivity. They were free, but they could not experience all of the freedom God had for them until they surrendered to Him.

The Lord continued to give them victories in spite of what they did. He would provide them with a victory and tell them to record the victory as a memorial. That meant as a reminder. I hope that you will use the journal along with this book and create a memorial, a reminder of all the times God has brought you out and delivered you and provided for you. Let this be a place of thanks that no matter how many cycles you entered or how many cycles you may enter – He won't give up on you. He didn't give up on me.

Real Stories from Real Survivors

The way everyone becomes a victim is different. I worked at a bank and was very naïve. I got caught up in a banking scam, and after I was cleared of involvement, I was left unemployed. So, I begin to think about dancing. It was really popular among young women at the time, and everyone always complimented me on my body and my looks. I thought it would be a quick way to make fast money and get on my feet. I was pretty sure I could control the situation. You can never control when another person takes over your life and forces you to surrender to them. I am an overcomer now, and I am thankful that I lived to tell my story. My experience in the game was short compared to others I know. I'm glad that I can help them by sharing my experience and supporting them to make good decisions for themselves without judgment. What gave me the strength to stay out of the game once I got out was the feeling I had while I was in. I never felt safe. Some people think it is easy to walk away or to just "stop" – it's not. Another girl who tried to leave was beaten so badly in front of me. The pimp she left with was murdered, and I was terrified. I never felt so objectified, I was just a piece of meat, and I never wanted to feel that way again.

A.L.

Grace the Fulfillment

Grace, the fulfillment is on the cusp of stepping over into the promised land. It is the time in your life when you are on your way to your *Exodus*, life is still happening around you, but you know that there is something greater pulling on you — drawing you to come out. It is the exhaustion with *the life* and the awareness of the promise that's to come.

I think about the building we use to support survivors and give them a place to stay. Before there was the building, I had the trunk of my car, before I had the trunk of my car, I had the thought in my mind. But before grace was fulfilled and the thought was in my mind, I had the pipe in my mouth, and before the pipe in my mouth - I was laying in the field, before I was laying in the field, I was in somebodies bed, before I was in somebodies bed, I was raped and before I was raped I was molested and before I was molested my parents divorced. All of this is grace fulfilled.

I say that it is not only grace fulfilled; it is the goodwill of God, his unmerited favor. Have you ever looked at everything you've gone through and wonder how is it that you are where you are right now? That you are who you are right now? That is a daily place of thanksgiving for me. Through all that time and all that I experienced, grace was being fulfilled because

God kept giving me chances. He didn't let me die. Even when I wanted to, He refused to allow it.

Every time that I should have been guilty, God showed up and fulfilled His grace. When I could have been trapped in my thoughts and still blaming other people, He changed my thought pattern. When you become stuck blaming others, it locks you in and denies you access to your *Exodus*. You have to be willing to allow Him to change how you think. I had to learn that God didn't even want me to blame myself. He didn't want me judging other people. He wanted me to let it all go. Let go of everything that was keeping me bound and to finally rest in His grace.

Resting in His grace and resting in His mercy was the fulfillment of grace in my life. This changed the way that I looked at myself and gave me the power to see myself as God saw me - through grace.

Distant Memories…

At this time in my life, I was well aware of how I made money. I learned the ropes, I took care of myself, and I was not ashamed of the lifestyle I lived. So when I started a relationship with him, he knew exactly who I was, and I knew who he was. When he returned, he had bags of lingerie and asked who would be willing to try it on. Of course, I was, and so I did. I was no longer afraid of anything. I had experienced almost everything, so I was operating in what I thought was full control. It was nothing for me to do what needed to be done, to get the attention, and to make money. I was *Live Wire* when I performed, and *Kim the Cutter* in the streets. I was taking care of me, finally. I tried the lingerie on and waited to see who wanted to make a purchase, and he stood up and said that I was all his. I know it is hard to understand, but being in *the life* and being treated so poorly, to have somebody want me, felt like real intimacy.

We stayed locked in a room for three days laughing, getting to know each other, using drugs, and having sex. It was a mini-vacation for me, and it became what we called a love affair for those three days. I remember his mom knocking on the door and asking him - *didn't I have somewhere to go*. His sister came home and questioned, "*isn't she supposed to go home?*" When I left out of that room, I was about 130 pounds soaking wet. I had been high for 3 or 4 days straight. He said he wanted to bring me out of the room and introduce me to his family. I never had a man say that to me. I went into the bathroom and tried to make myself look presentable. There was nothing, absolutely nothing presentable about how I looked. I remember biting on the eyeliner to try and get it to work. I was just so excited to meet his mom, even if it was the same mom that told him I needed to go home.

The crazy thing about this man is that after that experience, he would find me everywhere I went. He would find the drug dealers that sold me drugs and tell them not to sell drugs to me. He would look for me on the block. He wouldn't let anyone else have me, he would buy all of my time, and he kept saying he saw something in me. He saw something that no one else apparently had never seen, and he wanted to keep me all to himself. I liked the thought of someone wanting me to themselves. Unfortunately, he ended up going to jail, and when he went away, he didn't know I was pregnant and that we would have a son together.

There *really* is a Romeo part of the experience when you meet someone out on the street, and they change your life, they try to be for you what no one else has been, and that experience is real. For me, it was like God still giving me love and keeping me safe and moments to maintain my sanity and to keep me from living everyday suicidal. He knew what I needed. I remember one time he walked in during a drug transaction, and he smacked the drug dealer and told him that he knew not to sell me drugs. He blocked everything that I would try to do that could hurt me or cause damage. I wondered what his deal was. I figured maybe he wanted to sell me and was trying to get in good – but he didn't want to sell me at all, he wanted me to himself.

Had he not gone to jail, I'm not sure what would have happened. When he went away, I went back to my girl's dad. I wanted to try and make it work. I had a taste of what having one man could be like, and I wanted to make my girl's father that *one* man. I wanted to have a family and try sobriety again. When I went back to him I didn't know I was already pregnant with my other lover's son. When I had my son, the people around us tortured him, and they would call him the *imposter* because he didn't look like my girl's dad. I hated that he had to endure that. I hated that my brokenness created brokenness for him, a brokenness that he didn't deserve but was now forced to tolerate.

* * * *

Again there were stents of sobriety, but very little happiness. When I became pregnant with my baby daughter, I used and got high up until the day I had her. Her life is another example of the promises of God toward me and His grace. She is one of the smartest, most brilliant children that I know. She changed my life. I still look at my children and wonder why God loved me so much to give them to me. I didn't deserve their precious souls, but he allowed me to birth them into this earth. The way that they have forgiven me and loved me is only by the hand of a mighty God.

* * * *

Thoughts From The Biblical Exodus...

I want to reflect on Exodus Chapter 15 when Moses continued to sing of the love of God. He proclaimed that His unfailing love continued to lead the people ***He*** had redeemed. He declared the Lord will reign forever and ever. When I think of my children and the way the Father has allowed us to love each other through my journey and into my Exodus, I can sing of His love forever.

The song they wrote to the Lord was in the middle of what they were experiencing. It was their faith in how strong and mighty they believed God was and how they were counting on Him to bring them out. In the companion journal, I leave space for you to write a song to the Lord.

Moses and the children of Israel sang as they triumphed on the other side of the red sea. But before they got to the other side, the reality of the unknown hit them. They became reasonably afraid. I know what it feels like to have reasonable fear. Here it is God had delivered them, and their captors had come after them. The red sea was in front of them, and Pharaoh was behind them.

My Exodus has come with many moments of Pharaoh behind me (the temptation to cycle, the pain of the past), and the red sea in front of me. The red sea represents the fear of the future. Now that I'm free, what happens next? This fear can be so intense it can make you want to turn back.

Moses was confident in God. He knew that God's grace would be fulfilled toward them. He told the people in Exodus 14:13, "Do not be afraid. Stand still, and see the salvation of the Lord, which He will accomplish for you today for the Egyptians whom you have seen today; you will never see them again forever".

I have to tell you, that is one of my favorite passages of scripture. Moses wanted them to be clear that they would never see them again, ever. Needless to say, God brought them out beyond the red sea. I won't give you the details. I'll encourage you to read it.

Moses shared the word of the Lord with the children of Israel that if they listened carefully to the voice of the Lord and do the things that were right, He would keep them from the diseases that He brought upon the Egyptians. I know this keeping power; it has kept me.

Real Stories from Real Survivors

What made me "leave" my Trafficker (pimp) was two reasons. 1st- I realized there was no "love" left for me in this man. He proved to me that there was NO "love" left for me because of how he treated my son and me. 2nd My son was abused by his nephews, he never once tried to find healing or help for my son. I knew I had to find someone that could help my son. It wasn't about me anymore. It was about my baby boy. I didn't believe I deserved love, but I knew this child, that was innocent did. With this as motivation & the love of God helping me to find a "safe" way out of this trap that I was in. I'm so glad God gave me forever friends that loved me no matter what. They truly had "agape" love for me and my son. Back when I left "the life" there was NO term "trafficking." So there was no place to go for healing for me, but I kept trying to find help for my son. In time, God led me back to church, and He put people around me to nurture me in His love. Praise God for His agape love! He turned my life around. I not only found help for my son, but I found support for myself. I am forgiven, and I am worthy of His love. Through Him, I survived, and so did my miracle child! I thank God for connecting me with Nancy – she is such an encouragement for me when I need a little boost. She helps me to keep surviving. To thrive & survive!

D.D.

Real Stories from Real Survivors

I became a victim of sex trafficking by trusting a man who promised me the world. I became a survivor by putting my life in God's hands and bravely walking the road that felt right in my spirit but was so hard in my flesh. Today, I thrive. I use my gifts to help others, and I seek help when I need it. I am committed to becoming my best self so that I can leave a positive, beautiful mark on this world. I want it to be a blessing that Rachel Thomas Was Here.

Rachel Thomas
Author, Ending the Game Curriculum.
@rachelthomaswashere

The Exodus

The Reflection

Have you ever had that moment in your life that when you try to reflect on it, you don't even know what you're looking at. I know the Nancy I've become, and when I look back at the Nancy, I used to be, at the things that I never thought I would go through. For me it's the things I thought I would never get out of. For all of the time that I sat on the edge of a bed with a crack pipe in my mouth, I reflect on those things. When I look in the mirror, I no longer see that woman, but I do see the reflection of what she used to be.

That girl that did escort services, that was the pole dancer, the girl that was suicidal. The girl that changed her men like she changed her panties, one after the next, day after day, sometimes hour after hour. I lived trying to fill that void and fill that gap. The reflection of all those things has changed the way I look at the mirror and the way the mirror looks back at me. I often ask myself as I stare at my reflection, "what do you see now?" When I look in the mirror now, I see something I never thought I'd see before. I see strength, hope, and resilience. I see God in me. I don't see a broken woman or a broken girl. I see a warrior, a survivor, an advocate, a proud mom, a grandmother, I see an entrepreneur.

Most importantly, I see what God sees about me, that I am the apple of His eye. That I am fearfully and wonderfully made.

I won't tell you that sometimes I don't still see the scars because I do, but I'm not running from them anymore or denying them. I own the flaws that I had and the flaws that I have, and I surround myself in scripture and the truth of the Word of God. As you are coming into your *Exodus* the person you were will always try to resurface. That doesn't mean that you aren't walking into a new beginning. It's just a moment for you to reflect on what was and thank God for what is. It's not for you to get stuck, and please don't drown in condemnation and self-hate. That's not what God wants for you, and it only delays your exit.

Distant Memories...

By the time I had Destiny, I no longer wanted to be with their dad, and because she came from him, I didn't want her either. I didn't want another reminder of the pain he put me through, and I know this contributed to my drug use while being pregnant with her. Destiny is the baby that saved my life. She is the only one of my children that I named; somebody else named all of my other children. But this baby *I called Destiny*, and before they could move me on the birthing table, she was here, and social services took her away from me before I could even hold her. She was the child that made me want to get my life together. It is because of her I tried again, I believed again, and I got clean again.

Destiny was designed to do great things, and she did – she has. When they took her from me, she was the only thing I longed for. I never had a place of my own or a home for my children and me. I was always staying with family or with a man, but after her, I knew I needed a house. I wanted a home so that I could get my children back. So that I could give them what they deserved. I bought my first house at 4333 West Villard. I remember the day they brought my baby to the house in a van. I was excited like I never had children before. She was amazing. I had gone to drug rehab, I was getting my life in order, and I couldn't wait to have my baby back. I watched her take her first steps. She gave me back the moments I missed with my other children.

*　　*　　*　　*

I remember walking down to the White Residential program (a drug rehab facility that was in Milwaukee, Wisconsin); it was the last chance for me to get custody of my baby. I felt like it was the last chance for my *Destiny.* I missed my appointment with my case manager because I got high the day before and couldn't pull myself together. When I finally did, I was a day late, and I didn't have a way to get there, so I walked. I walked miles. When I showed up I told the case manager I was so sorry, I told her I would do whatever it took, but please, please give me another chance. I don't know why she did, but she did. I worked that program, I went to all of the groups they assigned, I did the work, I was willing to do whatever it took, to prove to them that I was a worthy mom. In doing all this, I knew that it was time for me to go home to my faith.

My life had so many lines of the blood of Christ, so many moments he stepped in to help me when I didn't even know it, and I knew I needed to return to God. To thank Him for keeping me safe during the abuse, for allowing me rest at the truck stop, even down to the day *sugar britches* took me home. God has always been there. He has always covered me and kept me. All the times, I thought I could do a little of this or a bit of that, and get away with it and be okay, God kept me.

I will tell anyone that has struggled with addiction to anything that you cannot have just a little. A little will always get you back in the cycle of addiction. Your body and your mind are already set up to long for the thing you were once addicted to, and any memory of it that you give a voluntary response too - is going to set you back.

Things kept getting better for me; I had my 2nd house built from the ground through a project with habitat for humanity. I remember turning the key in the door on a fall day in

September. Everybody had a bedroom to themselves. It was our home, our safe place to live, and to be a family. This house wasn't just important because I purchased a house, it was important because all of my children were there and it was ours.

I had a decent job, and I stopped using. I remember one day picking up my check from the office and opening it to realize I didn't have enough to cover my house payment and keep us with the things we needed. I broke down and cried. The thing about being in *the life,* if I needed more money – I could make more money. Trying to live a new life, I could not do this. I was so discouraged, and a lady that new my story asked me how short I was; I told her I needed $50 more dollars, and she took it out her purse and gave it to me. Again, the love of God was keeping me and providing for me.

I decided to marry the love of my life, and we were going to try and make it work, raise our children, and have a happy family. I never worried about him hurting me or about him not being faithful or true. My only worry was if he relapsed. While he was in jail, he got jailhouse salvation and said he was ready to serve the Lord. I'm not sure what made my sobriety an issue for him, but there was something about me being clean he didn't like.

He decided one night he wanted to go out, and I didn't want him to go alone; I wanted to be a good wife, so I went with him. I relapsed. I remember the drink that did it; it was a tequila sunrise. I was in my 30's, and I was back looking for drugs, they're never too hard to find. We found them, and I remember taking my first hit, and it felt so good, but before the high could settle in, the depression and shame hit me first. I dreaded the morning coming, and seeing what I had become, what I had done to myself again. I was too embarrassed to go home, so I got us a hotel room.

I remember my children calling and asking were we coming home. I tried hard to pull it back together, but you can't mess around and not get caught up. That one drink cost me years of my life. When I fully surrendered to God, He gave me the strength I needed to break the stronghold the high had in my life. After a while, no matter how hard I would try, I could not get high. I was thankful that the feeling and desire to use drugs was leaving my body. I knew to stay sober; I could not stay married to someone that was not committed to the process. I started visiting a church, and I realized I missed God so much. I kept fighting with the thought of going back to church, and he refused. I knew without God, and with his addiction, we could not stay married. We divorced.

* * * *

It wasn't long before I found myself needing to be with a man again. It wasn't sexual at all; I needed to be married so that I could feel like I belonged to something, to somebody. I wanted to know that somebody loved me. I had not entirely accepted that God loved me; there were parts of me that wondered how he felt about the lifestyle I once lived, and all of the things I had done. I figured if I didn't have approval from God, I could at least get approval from a man. I married another man that I figured would fill this void because he was a man of God.

Not before long, I realized I just swapped addictions. It was no longer to drugs or sex; it was to the need for love. I tried something different, and instead of marrying an older man, I married a younger man. When you have experienced so much pain, and your sexuality and womanhood have been this deeply wounded, you have to allow God to heal that before trying to build another relationship.

A man's love won't heal you; only God's love will. That marriage also ended in divorce. I had to get out, during one of our arguments I overheard my children praying to God asking Him not to let me go back in the streets because of what was happening in the marriage. I knew then I was done; I could not endure another emotional wrecking and have my children in fear that they would lose their mom again. They would not.

I took time after this relationship to *really* pour out to God and to welcome Him in, to be honest with Him about things that happened in my life, and to invite Him to heal my heart. I used the time I had to invest in my children and to become a community advocate while standing in the truth that I was a survivor. I finally had a conversation with God about the molestation, about the rape, about my parent's divorce, about my multiple divorces. I poured out to Him about everything, and to my surprise, He was not judgmental. He wasn't angry. He was listening.

* * * *

Thoughts From The Biblical Exodus...

Exodus 20:23 (NKJV) Do not make any gods alongside me; do not make for yourselves god of silver or gods of gold. As challenging as it was to come out, it can be even more challenging to stay out. You've read about my cycles. Sometimes they seem like too many. I would question what was wrong with me, and why couldn't I get it right. One of the reasons is those small gods that wanted my worship. They weren't gods of silver or gold, but this time, it was gods of sex and men – gods of acceptance, that kept me circling in the wilderness looking for these gods and not for God.

After the last relationship that almost sent me into a cycle, I realized I was strong enough not to return. I realized that the Egyptians I had seen for years before I would see no more; my heart was full of praise. It changed my relationship with God, and my prayer became the prayer of Exodus 33:13 (NKJV) – Lord, if you are pleased with me, teach me your ways so that I may know you and continue to find favor with you.

When that became my prayer, I knew I had stepped over into my Exodus. No matter what happened, what people said, what trials I experienced, as long as I could return to this place of prayer and petition. This place of crying God teach me your ways so that I can find favor with you. I finally wanted to be different, and I believed that He had the power to make me different. His power was making me different.

Yes, I spent time in the wilderness after my Exodus. Every moment in the wilderness, God was still with me. He was still keeping me and covering me. He was still speaking to me and telling me how much He loved me and how He desired for me to live a full and free life in the land He promised for me. God has a land promised for every person reading this book. The land He has promised for you is your destiny; it's where your peace is, and it's where you will find your purpose.

Real Stories from Real Survivors

I have gone from victim to survivor and now Certified Advocate for Domestic Violence & Sexual Assault. Domestic Violence was not anything I'd ever heard of as a child or young adult. I was preyed on during a devasting divorce that left me vulnerable, bored, fascinated with money, nice cars, and material things. When a perpetrator preys on you and offers you things you desire to feel better, it is easy to become sucked into a life of lies and pain. I now welcome the mission of God in my life, and I do everything I can to advocate for those that are still in danger. I love and honor ALL Survivors and never forget about those that have been lost. I am dedicated to supporting and providing resources to women who have been abused. Often when women are abused, they feel alone and think they don't have any help or support – I want them to know that they **do** have support, and as a fellow survivor, I want everyone to know that there can be success after abuse. There is an awesome God who will provide everything you need! What seems like the end can become a new beginning.

C.M.

Eternity Forever

So why *eternity forever?* Eternity forever is that eternal hope that the bible speaks of, the promise of eternal life, and that is what I now have. It's when you can see the broken pieces of your life start to make sense, and you can embrace the *Genesis* without shame. For me, it was when I got back on the Potter's wheel, and God shaped me over again from darkness to light. You can see the picture He designed for your life manifest in front of you. All of the parts begin to fill itself in, and I realized the hurt, pain, drug addiction, all the trauma and drama in my life have worked for my good.

My life has become so dreamlike, and all the things I ever imagined that I could be, I am becoming. I never thought that one day, I would be able to stand on the shoulders of my pain and reach up to heaven and receive. I can receive all of the blessings that God has promised me. I can reach up and embrace all that I have experienced, and know it is now okay, and that all of it is for the glory of God.

For me, it is an eternal prophetic existence that declares I never have to go back. I never have to be the woman I was. I never have to experience the chains on my heart again. I cycled so much trying to fully walk into my *Exodus* and this place that I'm in now, I know that no one can take me back. I realized that once I said yes entirely to God that I never had to go back.

I no longer have to be bound. I am free. The way I thought about myself has changed, and this change is forever.

When I go back and think about the *Genesis*, eternity becomes the *Genesis* in that I am right back on track with the way God intended me to go. He has brought a new beginning into my life. He made all things new. Every single thing about my life is different. This is where my ***new beginnings*** happened.

I realized that all things worked together for my *Exodus*. The future is brighter than I ever thought it would be. Even writing this book and sharing my story with you – it is no longer just a thought, but it is pen and paper into your hands. It is decades of tears, and trauma turned into triumph. It's the letter I wrote in the 8th grade to my mother, promising her that I would make her proud. It is the Lord fulfilling His promises in my life and allowing me to fulfill my promise to her.

I believe everything I've gone through was for something; everything I've experienced was for this moment, for this *Exodus*. I started Fresh Start Learning where our mission is to strengthen families, restore the underprivileged people of society, and rebuild communities. We are committed to advocating and raising awareness of social justice issues by strategically creating social development programs to transform the lives of those we serve and their environments.

Who would have ever imagined that I, the girl whose journey is written on the pages of this book, would be the woman of God that I am now? Certainly not me, but God knew it from the very beginning. He always planned to bring me out, and if you are reading this book and still trapped in a life you never wanted to live – He will bring you out too.

Coming out is never easy. Sometimes there is nowhere to go, and there is no one to go to. I burned so many bridges during my cycles that there were times I really needed help, but those that were exhausted with my struggle were no longer there to help me. The pain of nowhere to go is why I developed Humble Beginnings Drop-in Spot. It is a temporary shelter for women to come off the street, have a hot shower, a good meal, and a soft bed to sleep in. We provide cozy pajamas and fuzzy socks, food, and the Word. When the women get ready to leave the next day, they are equipped with resources to continue on their survivor journey. I can't fix their problems overnight, but I know the hope a peaceful sleep and a good night's rest can provide. *The life* I lived taught me that one good night of sleep could be the change you need to change your life. I am blessed to offer this change to women.

While I understand that not all women will come in from the street, I committed to going to them. Every stage in my life where I experienced a void, where there were moments I needed someone, I endeavored in my heart to create a service to fill that need. Purpose Filled Purses is another initiative at the heart of eternity forever. For the women that are not ready to come in, I go out. I meet them where they are and provide them a purse full of things I know they need. I know what they need because I know what I needed. I know it is the smallest gesture of love that reminds them that they are human.

I live in a region described as the hub of sex trafficking. Let me be specific when I say the hub; it is in the top five in the nation for consecutive years in a row. The purpose in each purse includes bibles, deodorant, perfume, socks, toothpaste, toothbrushes, and other hygiene products. God gave me this idea as a service to give to those who share the journey I was on and to be a guiding light toward their *Exodus*. I know those moments where you want to commit suicide; you just want to end it all. I ask God to help me intentionally find women that are in that moment and allow me to give them hope.

The most important thing in the purse is a letter of love, that is the true purpose. Simple words that transform lives are written on these notes. They are handwritten with words like "don't forget that you are strong and beautiful." I will never forget one lady I met and approached her to pick out a purse; she asked me how much it was. When I told her it was free, she broke down in tears. I knew those tears because, in *the life*, nothing is free. I know if someone had walked up to me with one of those purses, it would have given me hope, given me life, and led me closer to my *Exodus.*

*   *   *   *

My Present & Future...

Fresh Start Learning was born out of me getting my children back and wanting to make up for the years I missed with them. I wanted to know everything there was to know about children. I became a trainer for childcare agencies. I started teaching classes for those that worked as daycare providers. My children are the reason Fresh Start Learning exists.

I only started the advocacy work after my second divorce when I heard my children whispering their prayers to God about not wanting me to go back into the street because of how I was being treated. I cried out to God and told Him I needed Him right away, and He was there. He gave me strength and courage; He helped me find my voice and then put His strength on my voice to be an advocate for others. That's where the advocacy was birthed. I first had to learn to advocate for myself so that I could be used to advocate for others.

I was facilitating training for a childcare agency, and a woman raised her hand and asked what can she do with the pain of being molested by her brother from childhood to adulthood. I begin to minister to her in the training. I opened up and shared my story with her and told her about the healing power of Jesus Christ. It is moments like those; God would breathe new businesses and new programs into my soul. He created these things in the middle of everything that I was going through, and He had a plan on how He would use it. I had no idea my life would be a living testament for what I've been through. In all of it, God was steadfast and consistent in my life.

He showed His faithfulness in the lives of my children. My son prayed for me when I could not pray for myself. My mom told me he would walk around the room and call the name "Jesus" over and over; he knew as a kid, there was power in that name. Even now my son calls me the modern-day Harriet Tubman. He thinks I'm brave for going to get other women from the captivity of sex trafficking. The thing that makes it such a big compliment is that it's coming from, *my* son. He is one of my biggest cheerleaders. It's changed my life to watch him succeed. To know that he loves me anyway. To think that He has been alive 33 years of my life. He has witnessed many of the cycles and suffered through some of the worst, and yet he loves me. He is just another example and proof the hand of God is orchestrating my life.

My oldest daughter has four children, all kings. She witnessed abuse and has seen some of the same trauma I have, and she is one of the strongest women I know. She is the best mom to her children, with one man, and was bold enough to move to a new state to make a better life for her family. She is the epitome of what a mother should be; I'm so proud of her. She tells me how much I inspire her, but the truth is she *really* inspires me. Even when you think your children are not watching you, they're watching.

My last three children, although they didn't see the worst of my life, I still couldn't love them right because I was trying so hard to make up for lost time, working so hard to do it right. I was so strict on them. I just wanted them to have more than I did, to be more than I was. I would have given my life for my children, and I still will. They deserve the best that God has to offer them, and I'm so thankful He has allowed me to see His goodness through them before I leave this earth.

My son, I call my love child, lost his dad before he could have a relationship with him. I wish he could have gotten to know the type of man his father was to help him understand the kind of man he is. He is so courageous and dependable. His heart can immediately pick up on what's going on, and he wants to find a way to make it better. I am so proud of him and the man he has become. He always tells me that he learned his strength from me, not even knowing that I got my strength from being a mother to him.

My next daughter is my mini-me because she has my heart. She is the emotional part of me because I took her everywhere I went. She has a heart like no one else I know. When she was little, no one wanted to keep her because she was so attached to me. She was the extension of God's grace with me everywhere I went, and I didn't even know it. No matter where I left her, she would tell people, "my mom is coming back for me." She never gave up on me. I love her because she gave me something I didn't even know could exist, and that was unconditional love. She wanted *me,* remember the pain of not being wanted and not being desired – but this little girl wanted *me* to be her mom, and she made sure everyone knew it.

My baby girl. I named her in prophetic hope of what God would do in my life. I didn't even know it at the time. I was still too far gone to *really* believe in what I spoke over her, but I spoke it anyway. Calling her Destiny wasn't by accident. It was by divine assignment for her life and mine.

Now, years later, I'm the Executive Director of Fresh Start, having all of the things God gave me over ten years ago coming into existence. I think about the girls that still reach out to me. Girls whose lives I've been able to impact. It's well over 200 girls I've been able to serve on a one on one basis, thousands of lives I've been able to reach from platforms, telling my journey. I know that my journey has been set by God himself.

Jeremiah 29:11 (NKJV) is one of my favorite scriptures because it says that God knows the plans He has for our life. I know this is just the beginning. My Exodus is now the new beginning of my life. Writing this book was one of the most challenging things I've ever done, I haven't been down this journey in so many years. I haven't been down this road in so long. I haven't looked into the closets of my pain, because sometimes things hurt us so deeply that we want to forget – but you have to remember. You have to go back and remember so that you can reach out and empower someone else. That was the purpose of sharing my Exodus with you; that was my heart. To share with you what God has done for me. I know there are broken spirits waiting for someone to show them an Exodus. I said to God "here am I – I'll be the one. Use my life to show people your glory."

That's exactly what He's doing. None of this is about me; it's all because of Him. God. My Lord and Savior, Jesus Christ.

* * * *

When I think about eternity forever, sometimes it's too much to absorb. There are two parts of that forever, and one includes the sadness of losing loved ones like my mom and people that were really close to me. The joyous part is that I know I never have to go back to the old lifestyle, the hurt and the pain that almost destroyed me. To know that in eternity forever is my *Exodus* and it is creating beautiful memories for me. I think of a song that mentions not going to heaven with my life full but going to heaven and leaving an eternal footprint here on earth.

When my mom passed I learned so much about her. I learned that much of her life had been shaped by her Genesis, that she never had the experience of being mothered and loved the way she needed, she gave me the best she had. When I was in the eighth grade and before things took a sharp turn, I wrote a letter to my mom, and I told her that I would make her proud. I was acting out and apologized to her and promised her that I would do better. When she died, the letter I wrote to her was tucked away in her bible. She placed my words to her inside of the most precious things she owned, the Word of God.

It's funny when I think about have I arrived now that I've bought my first car? My first home? I've had a chance to speak before thousands! I've won so many awards, and I know that there are more to come. Amid the celebration, the Father reminds me that I am back at the *Genesis* and that there is more to come. When I am heavy with the reality of my experiences He offers me a new grace and mercy every day. When I make mistakes, the mistakes from my yesterday no longer have to enter into my today. I get a clean slate every day! Wow! Guess what? So do you.

*   *   *   *

Thoughts From The Biblical Exodus…

You know the promised land I mentioned in the last chapter. That is my eternity forever; that is where I live and dwell with God, my Father. He uses me from this place. He allows me to rest in this place. He gives me His grace in this place. It is everything I've ever dreamed of and more!

I'm overwhelmed that after all I've gone through, all I've done, all I've experienced that such a gracious and great God LOVES ***me.*** Did you get that? After everything written in this book, He called me out into an Exodus, He's given me a new beginning, and He calls me His beloved. A name I thought I'd never be able to embrace, but I wear it as a badge. I wear it as a sign of His redemptive love. He calls you His beloved as well. We are HIS.

Exodus 34:6 (NKJV) And the Lord passed before him and proclaimed, "The Lord, the Lord God, merciful and gracious, longsuffering, and abounding in goodness and truth.

Real Stories from Real Survivors

This. Is. My. *Exodus.* I remember when I started to like me again, when I could trust me again, believe in me again. Eventually, I began to feel again. It was the first time I could look at myself in the mirror without crying, without complaining, without criticism, free of concerns, because I started to see what I'm becoming. I realized that the old indeed is passing away and behold all things are becoming new. I see how I respond differently to others, how my love language has changed, how I don't look for payment for services of love, but I now love to serve others. My *Exodus* is in motion, but my new journey has just begun.

I am Nancy Yarbrough-Banks and This. Is. My. *Exodus.* – Where New Beginnings Happened. So ***where*** do we go from here? We follow the God Plan, which includes The Survivor Series. Be sure to stay connected so that you can witness more real stories from real survivors as I journey with them to their *Exodus.* I'm a phone call or email away, and I'd love to share more of my journey with you. Visit me online at freshstartlearninginc.org